CRACKING THE AMAZON INTERVIEW

BONUS MATERIAL

As a gift to all my readers I've created a free PDF of 127 resources for your job search, along with a step-by-step guide to create a great LinkedIn profile. The PDFs include resume templates, time management tools and apps to supercharge your job search.

Please visit here to download the PDFs:
https://mishayurchenko.me/127tools/

TABLE OF CONTENTS

INTRODUCTION

"Amazon.com receives thousands of resumes every week, from talented people all over the world. Our challenge is to find the very best and recruit them into one of the many challenging positions we offer. Setting the bar high in our approach to hiring has been, and will continue to be, the single most important element of Amazon.com's success. During our hiring meetings, we ask people to consider three questions before making a decision:

- Will you admire this person?
- Will this person raise the average level of effectiveness of the group they're entering?
- Along what dimension might this person be a superstar?"

Jeff Bezos, Amazon Founder and CEO

* * * * *

I spent four years recruiting top talent for Amazon as an agency partner. I met with hundreds of job seekers, prepared them for interviews, and helped many of them find jobs. During that time I was able to gather feedback from hiring managers and job seekers alike, observe interview styles, and figure out what worked and what failed. This has given me a unique perspective on the company, and I'm excited to share what I learned so that you have the resources you need to succeed.

While I cannot predict every question that Amazon will ask in an interview, I can say that the process is fairly structured. This makes the interview process transparent and easy to prepare for because we know many of the themes they will cover and questions they will ask. Imagine if your teacher in university told you most of the questions that were going to be on the test beforehand - all you would have to do is practice. Consider this book your study guide.

As a result of this structured interview process, many job seekers who do poorly in interviews simply do not spend enough time preparing. And often, the ones who do spend time preparing do not spend enough time focusing on the right things. I compiled information about the Company's interview process, questions, and techniques that have been most successful for former applicants (current Amazon employees). This mini-guide will walk you through what it takes to get through an Amazon interview, step by step. All you have to do is read and prepare.

WHO DOES AMAZON HIRE?

Amazon is a massive company with more than half a million employees across the globe. While every department, position, and even culture is going to favor different personalities and skillsets, I find that most people that work at Amazon have these three qualities:

1. Logical/analytical thinking skills
2. Hunger for growth
3. Desire for continuing career development or just "not at the peak of their career yet"

From a consumer perspective, we see Amazon as an amazing company that has taken over the world to provide us with services that have changed our lives for the better. But what does it take to run this beast of an organization? The speed of business, the innovation, and the big thinking come at a price. The culture largely stems from the leadership principles which I will discuss in Chapter 6, but, like most companies, Amazon's culture is largely influenced by CEO Jeff Bezos.

Jeff is known to challenge ideas very aggressively. The customer always, always, *always* comes first. He brings an empty chair to meetings just to remind people of this fact. Often arguments get heated party because his standards are, for many, unimaginably high.

Unsurprisingly, Amazon received harsh criticism from the media after a New York Times article came out with stories portraying the culture as 'combative and hostile' -- not to mention the grueling hours. The standards are unreasonably high, and performance reviews are notoriously competitive. Jeff Bezos didn't completely deny this, and from my own experience, I know that there is some truth in these claims. Of course, Amazon has taken steps to improve their working environment and culture -- starting with the introduction of flex time and other HR initiatives.

However, it's important to take a step back and understand the implications of Amazon's Bezos-led culture.

Amazon is largely compared to other tech companies like Google and Facebook who are known for their casual work environments, flex-time, and people-centric mindsets. When viewed through this lens, Amazon looks like the odd (and mean) kid on the block.

Although it's a matter of perspective, Amazon is not for the faint of heart. If you are looking for a cushy job or just a change of scenery you will likely be torn apart in the company. While this culture is not "bad," teams at Amazon compete with each other, growth/scalability is emphasized, and slowing down is not an option. That's what happens when you are trying to change the world.

I know people who *love* working at Amazon and others who left after three months. I know parents who work from home half the time and others who stay in the office late every day. It's important to remember that culture changes depending on the business, team, and manager. Some bosses are going to be more strict than others, and some people are also going to join the company with a level of maturity and ability to manage their team.

Amazon tends to favor people who have shown their ability to solve real problems, and you will find you will be solving new problems every day. Amazon is a great company to join if you are interested in creating your own startup in the future. It's also a great company to join if you have *already* had experience running a startup. Whether you were successful or not, Amazon sees value in those who have fallen into the depths of failure and climbed their way back out. You will often hear the business itself described as an oversized startup. The teams are lean, efficient and follow what Jeff Bezos refers to as the "two pizza rule," meaning that a team should never be so big that they need to order more than two pizzas.

Regardless of what position you are in, you will always have to deal with a certain amount of data and numbers. People who are not comfortable with this either adapt quickly, get stuck, or never get the job. If you like numbers, you have an advantage, but don't be intimidated by the thought of hardcore data analysis or machine learning. Your role includes everything from weekly reporting of sales results using Excel or using historical data to convince a senior VP to give you a larger marketing budget. If you can adapt and learn quickly, data and numbers will be a valuable tool, not a career roadblock.

Amazon's products and services are rarely geared towards small markets. Usually, you'll be working with a national or global user base. This means you'll need to come up with innovative ways to scale services without spending too much money. You will meet many great leaders and mentors who will help you learn along the way, but no one will hold your hand. You need to take ownership of your own growth and embrace Amazon's distinct culture.

In conclusion, if you are looking for a big growth opportunity to lead a big project, build new skills, scale a business, manage a big team, or stretch yourself —then Amazon is the right company for you. Amazon tends to push people to try new things and go beyond their main responsibilities, despite what their job descriptions may say. People who want to stay very focused on one job role and skillset might find it hard to juggle all the responsibilities.

CHAPTER 1:

THE FLYWHEEL

"Bezos and his lieutenants sketched their own virtuous cycle, which they believed powered their business. It went something like this: lower prices led to more customer visits. More customers increased the volume of sales and attracted more commission-paying third-party sellers to the site. That allowed Amazon to get more out of fixed costs like the fulfillment centers and the servers needed to run the website. This greater efficiency then enabled Amazon to lower prices further. Feed any part of this flywheel, they reasoned, and it should accelerate the loop."

- Brad Stone, The Everything Store

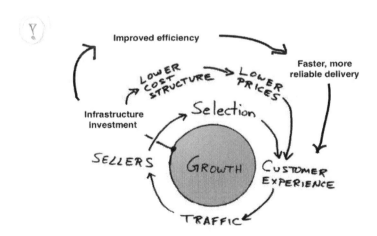

In order to understand the interview process, it is important to first understand the basics of the Amazon business model that has propelled them to such amazing heights. Their "flywheel" business model represents how Amazon operates at all levels of the organization. Once you have a firm understanding of how the Company functions, it will guide *how* you answer interview questions.

To begin, I will define each part of the Amazon business model:

- *Selection* - Consider the number of products and services available on Amazon.com - it is nearly infinite! This variety also applies to different categories, like the selection of Kindle content or number of movies made available on Prime Video.
- *Sellers* - As with the selection, there are many third-party sellers on the e-commerce platform. Amazon directly buys and sells products with these third-party vendors as a part of their business, but anyone (including you or me) is permitted to sell products on the site.
- *Customer Experience* - Amazon uses the metric of "lifetime customer value" or "LCV" to measure the customer experience. LCV = (Average Value of a Sale) * (Number of Repeat Transactions) * (Average Retention Time in Months or Years for a Typical Customer)
- *Lower Cost Structure* - By selling products online, Amazon does not incur costs of running physical "brick and mortar" shops. Thus, the Company runs a more scalable and cheaper business model than most retail companies.
- *Lower Prices* - Jeff Bezos, founder and CEO of Amazon, believes that customers will always want lower prices. It is one of the few "timeless truths."
- *Traffic* - This simply refers to the number of users driven to Amazon.com.

Every component of the flywheel is an accelerator. When effort is put into any one of these areas, it positively impacts all of the other components.

For example, as the Company attracts more sellers to the website, this will increase the selection of products. In turn, this will lead to a better customer experience and an increase in future traffic, which distributes more energy to the rest of the flywheel.

All of this leads to growth and a faster spinning flywheel (represented by "growth" in the center).

What you'll also notice on the flywheel is that there is no circle for "take profits." Indeed, Amazon is renowned for reinvesting its profits into new businesses, warehouses, and fulfillment centers. While this might upset shareholders in the short term, it is a proven and extremely successful long-term strategy. If you want to dive deeper into Amazon's financial model and growth strategy, take a look at Ben Evan's analysis at this link: https://www.ben-evans.com/ benedictevans/ 2014/9/4/why-amazon-has-no-profits-and-why-it-works".

The Flywheel model in interviews

This flywheel is a fundamental concept to understand because everything Amazon does at a micro and macro level is connected to the flywheel. Corporate values are based on this model. The decision-making process is based on this model. When you go into an interview, you should be able to comfortably explain the flywheel model and understand how it shapes Amazon's operations.

It's imperative to keep the flywheel in mind when answering any interview question. When you receive questions about lowering prices or increasing website traffic, the questions may initially seem daunting and difficult to answer - they are not. Bring to mind the flywheel, and you will find your answer.

For example, if you are asked, *"How would you increase traffic to the Baby Goods category?"*, simply bring to mind the other parts of the flywheel. The answer is one of one of the following: increasing the number of sellers, increasing selection, lowering prices, improving the customer experience, and lowering the cost structure — or a mix of all of these.

With that in mind, your answer could be "Let's lower the prices for our top 10 baby good items and run an advertising campaign for 1 week."

It is useful to spend some time thinking about the overall business and exploring their website and apps. Even if you are a frequent Amazon user, you might not have thought about how they monetize, yet manage to maintain such low prices. One of the company's mantras is to focus on long-term growth rather than short-term profit. This is why Amazon keeps reinvesting their revenues and starting new businesses. They have managed to build a huge business without actually being profitable.

As an exercise, I encourage you to check out Amazon's home page and browse through their categories. Look at the selection of their products, promotions they are running, and new products. Then put yourself in the shoes of an Amazon employee. Ask yourself the following questions: *"How are they driving traffic? How could I improve the selection? How do we maintain low prices for this product or category? How does this product fit into the larger ecosystem of services? What do we need in order to scale this part of the business?"*

Amazon is constantly experimenting with new businesses. Some have not taken off -- like the Amazon Appstore, while other businesses dominate industry categories (AWS, Kindle, etc.). Every business has a slightly different business model, revenue model, and customer. Customers can be consumers, businesses, entrepreneurs, sellers, and so forth in infinite variations. In any case, **remember that the flywheel applies to all of their businesses.**

Finally, use this understanding of the flywheel to better understand the job for which you are applying. Considering the job you are interested in, imagine how *your* position and role in the company would fit into the overall flywheel model. Use this to create smarter and more relevant questions which will impress the interviewer. **Whenever you get stumped on a question, always take your mind back to the flywheel.**

Now that we understand how the business works, I will discuss different levels of the overall organizational structure.

CHAPTER 2:

ORGANIZATIONAL STRUCTURE

Amazon has a job leveling system that determines your salary and seniority within the organization. With each level comes certain expectations. L stands for "level," with L1 being the lowest and L12 being the highest, currently occupied by the CEO, Jeff Bezos.

Below is a general guideline for the expectations and salaries of each level. However, keep in mind these numbers are not set in stone. Each department will have different budgets, and I have seen the numbers vary widely. For example, an L7 could be making an L8 salary, depending on the employee's experience, skill set, expertise and the department budget.

At first glance, the titles attributed to these levels can be misleading. Many people who have CEO and VP titles in their previous jobs end up joining as directors at Amazon. Many directors and VPs end up joining as senior managers. Why? Simply because Amazon is a global beast and the size of each business unit is enormous. Perhaps someone had a very senior title at their previous company, but it is unlikely that they were managing the same volume of work.

Do not get too tied up about the title and certainly do not let that prevent you from applying for a job. It is best to leave your ego at the door, at least until you have a deeper understanding of the job. Instead, take an opportunity to talk to Amazon HR and hiring managers to fully understand the *scope* of the job. Then decide if it is something worth applying for.

Here is a breakdown of the levels, titles, and sample job descriptions.

L1 - L3: The first three levels are contractors, hourly workers, and part-timers. Here's an example at L2-L3 level. These salaries can vary from minimum wage to 30-50k per year.

Data Center Associate (Contractor)
Job ID: 426969 | Amazon Data Services Japan K K

DESCRIPTION
- Effectively troubleshoot and repair servers and networks
- Manage all aspect of a mission critical spare parts pool for server and network equipment
- Various hardware troubleshooting and replacement
- Server and networking equipment installation and removal
- Responsible for the RMA and repair process for all devices
- Support senior technicians in daily works and activities as directed
- Directed project work

BASIC QUALIFICATIONS
- Bachelor or Junior College' degree, Bachelor's degree is preferred
- Relevant educational qualification majoring in Computer Science, Network Engineering, Electronic Engineering, Automation, and other Information Technology subject
- Basic Hardware Concepts on server, storage and network
- Understanding of basic computer/network concepts and terms
- Experience in Microsoft office applications including but not limited to Outlook, MS Word, and MS Excel
- Good English written and read skills (TOEIC +650 or equivalent knowledge)

PREFERRED QUALIFICATIONS
- Familiar with Linux operating system.
- Experience of networking setup and configuration.
- Experience of server operation system level development, familiar with server hardware.

L4 - Associate/Consultant level. Most college graduates enter at this level. In engineering terms, you would be a Software Development Engineer or SDE. This is a full-time salaried position, as are all levels from this point upward. The salary range is from $40-90k.

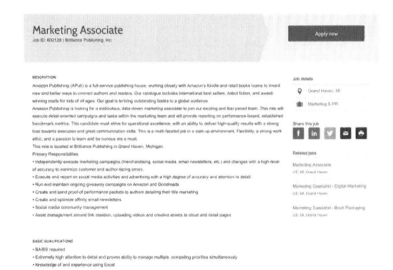

L5 - Manager level. You could be managing a small team or act as an individual contributor. $80-150k salary range.

L6 - Senior Manager level. You are likely going to be managing a team, but there are some individual contributors at this level. This is a senior level and requires you to work on complex projects and interact with directors, VPs, and senior stakeholders. The salary range is $120-250k.

SDE II

base

$150 - 181 avg $160

GBP 120 - 160k

x stock $275 - 625 avg 3/5

$155 base 175 stock

mvir

135 stocks

14

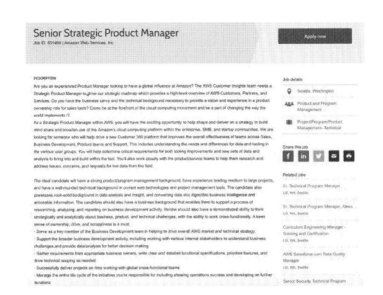

L7 - Sr. Manager/Principal/Director level. This is a big step up from L6 and usually involves managing a large organization. Salaries can range from 300-800k USD.

L8 - Director/GM level. A director could be managing a multi-million/billion dollar business unit and leading a cross-functional or 50+ person team. Or they could be starting up a new business, with the expectation of scaling it significantly. The salary range is $300k-1m USD+.

L9 - Interestingly, this level doesn't exist. Amazon purposefully left it out...the mystery remains.

L10 - VPs. They will be managing several directors in one country and/or globally. Most have been CEOs or GMs in their previous jobs. The salaries are from $1m USD upwards (jobs at this level are not listed online as Amazon usually directly sources interviewees).

L11 - SVPs. The "S" team or "SVP" title. Senior VPs that are overseeing global businesses. The salaries range from $2m USD upwards. (Again, this level of hire is not listed online as they usually directly source people).

L12 - Jeff Bezos. Net worth $100 billion +

While Amazon does not disclose the leveling of positions on their website, you can take the examples above to give you a rough idea of the ranges. Once you get an actual interview, you can ask the hiring manager what the of level the job is.

You can find a list of jobs that Amazon currently has available open here: https://www.amazon.jobs/

CHAPTER 3:

SUPERCHARGING YOUR RESUME

Amazon HR and hiring managers are going to skim over your resume and make a snap judgment within two seconds. They will either get excited by your resume or they will move on to the next one. In reality, the reason your resume doesn't get noticed is that job seekers don't know what companies want to see in a resume. There's a disconnect between what you think they want and what they really want.

Job postings can ask for many things, but when a hiring manager is perusing your resume it boils down to two things:

1. Specific keywords which fit their perception of the "ideal fit" for the position.
2. A sense of familiarity and "culture fit" with their company. Like everything in the interview process, the leadership principles play a huge role.

Let's explore these in more detail.

#1. Specific Keywords

Amazon wants to hire **logical, analytical, and humble employees that are comfortable with failure.**

Think about this for a second. *How can you highlight these traits in your resume?* Simply including numbers and certain keywords in your resume are going to go a long way. The easiest way to do this before applying at Amazon, pick out some of the keywords in the job description and pepper them into your resume. Of course, you should always be realistic and truthful.

Amazon uses their own jargon (like "dive deep" or "think big"), so it is useful to include similar language that not only to show your capability but also to build a sense of familiarity with the hiring manager/HR who is reviewing your resume.

I analyzed over 200 resumes that are publicly available on LinkedIn to find out which keywords Amazon employees tend to use in describing their previous jobs.

Keywords that Amazon loves to see on resumes:

- Go-to market strategy
- Go-to market
- Conversions
- Strategic
- Target vs. Actual
- ROI (Return on Investment)
- Analytics
- Data analysis
- Process improvement
- P/L Management (profit and loss)
- Built/designed/launched/developed

This does not mean you should frantically try and stuff in all of these words into your resume. Rather, think about your achievements and see if you can:

A. get more granular about the details and add numbers;
B. think about replacing or adding some words on your resume that accurately reflect your achievements with the words above.

While you may not specifically have experience managing a business unit and therefore cannot (and should not) include "P/L," you can still include other keywords. You can also show how you had an impact on your previous job or role. You should also <u>always include</u> <u>numbers in your resume.</u> At the minimum, include numbers related to money (sales/ marketing/finance) and/or the budget for a project you worked on. If you have specific numbers about a company's or team's overall size (number of employees, revenue, profit), then you should also include this information. This will give the interviewer a better idea of the scope of what you did, and it will be easier for them to imagine your previous role.

Lastly, a great way to get a feel for what kind of profiles Amazon is looking for is to go on Linkedin and look at the profiles of people already working there.

#2. Culture Fit

Amazon's culture centers around a series of leadership principles. I have listed the leadership principles in the section below with real examples of questions you'll be asked in the interview. However, you could and should also sprinkle in words from Amazon's principles and try to describe your achievements through the lens of these principles.

Specifically, you could include a combination of the following words that reflect their culture to make yourself sound more like an Amazonian:

- Customer-centricity
- Long-term growth
- Innovative
- Curiosity
- Track record of hiring

19

- Long-term vision
- Fast-paced
- Resourcefulness/frugality
- Stakeholder influence and pushback
- Results-driven

While some of these may seem pretty standard, they do reflect a lot of Amazon's specific values. I'd encourage you to think about times in your career where you've been able to demonstrate the above.

Common Resume Pitfalls to Avoid:

a) Many resumes are discarded for unprofessional email addresses. It's simple, but HR managers take notice. Make sure not to include works like "handsome, dashing, lover, friend, boy, gbc, xyz, 123." A safe email address is some format of your name. Gmail has automatic suggestions that are usually professional.

b) Do not include a photo on your resume. It is not necessary and while we expect people not to discriminate, some of the "diversity" requirements are not going to be advantageous for everyone.

c) "Reference will be provided on request" -- Don't write this on your resume as it's a waste of space; if you are going to provide a reference then go ahead and do it in the resume.

d) Do not use fancy fonts, with different colors and different sizes across entire resume (unless perhaps you are applying for a design position!)

e) Don't be afraid to mention achievements that you think might be unnecessary; often times extracurricular activities/volunteer experience can be a starting point for conversations in the interview.

Lastly, a professional LinkedIn profile is going to be crucial. Please visit the following link to download the full 60-page guide to creating your profile:

https://mishayurchenko.me/127tools/

CHAPTER 4:

DIRECT APPLICATIONS VS. RECRUITERS

When you submit your resume to Amazon, you'll either do so directly through their website (or LinkedIn), or you'll use an external recruitment agency which will present your application on your behalf. There are pros and cons to both, but generally speaking, I believe that if you can find a very good external recruiter who has a proven track record of helping and introducing job seekers to Amazon, you're likely to be better off.

Amazon has a strict and archaic HR policy called the "Ownership Policy" which basically states that your application is held hostage for six months by whoever sends it first. For example, if you submit your resume to Amazon directly, then only Amazon's internal HR can speak to you about that specific role for the following six months (from the date you pressed "send"). This means that even if a great recruiter approaches you with a job that seems more interesting, you have no choice but to continue speaking to Amazon's HR.

It goes both ways, of course. If you send your application through an external recruiter, then you have to continue interviewing through that specific recruiter -- you can't submit your resume to a different recruitment company for six months!

Thus it's important to choose your path wisely, lest you have your resume locked in.

To help you better decide, let's go through the advantages and disadvantages of each approach.

Direct Application

Pros	Cons
There are fewer chances for miscommunication that could arise from having a middleman (recruiter).	Even after your interview, the feedback will likely be thin as Amazon HR and internal recruiters tend to be quite vague with this information.
You won't feel any pressure from external recruiters trying to push you through the interview process.	You may never get feedback on your resume and/or your resume is never reviewed by HR because they're too busy.
You can apply for whatever role you'd like, not just taking the (possibly limited) "suggestion" of a recruiter	You will have very limited information about the interview process and interviewers, as Amazon's internal recruitment team doesn't spend much time preparing job seekers.

Recruiters

Pros	Cons
They can help you prepare for interviews and give you helpful advice that you wouldn't get from Amazon's HR.	Once you apply through one recruiter, you have to stick with them for the six month ownership policy.
They can control the speed of the interview process, negotiate your salary, and give	Recruiters are often trying to fill one specific position, so the number of jobs they present to

you perspective on the organization beyond one specific role.	you could be limited/ biased.
They can give you constructive feedback/advice on your resume and interviews.	If the recruiter has a poor relationship with Amazon, it could hinder or slow down your application process

The caveat with this "pro and con" analysis is that using a good recruiter with a strong relationship with Amazon is almost always going to be a better option than applying directly. They will have access to all open opportunities, can prepare you for interviews, negotiate your salary, manage the interview timeline, and have a financial incentive to get you hired!

The challenge is finding a good recruiter that has a strong connection with Amazon. **Here are a few key questions you can ask each recruiter to weed out the good from the bad:**

1. Have you met the hiring manager? Can you tell me about them, what is their personality like? What is their interview style and what are they really lookingfor?
2. What is *your* relationship like with the hiring manager?
3. Have you ever had anyone interview there before or made any successful placements? Can you describe the interview process? What are the names of the interviewers and what are their roles?
4. Can you explain the business model of the company? Who are their clients? How many users do they have?
5. Can you tell me about the position? Who else is on the team? What are their specific functions and responsibilities?
6. How would my performance be measured on the job?
7. Why is the job open - is it a new job or a replacement? How long has the position been open?

8. What is the career path for this role?
9. What is the growth plan of the department over the next couple of years?
10. Why do you think this is a good opportunity, considering my experience?

I suspect that some recruiters won't even bother getting back to you after seeing these questions. However, the good recruiters will have detailed answers and even likely schedule a phone call or face to face with you to go over every single question.

The best recruiter will answer all of your questions in great detail, have a strong relationship with the hiring manager, and will follow up with you to understand *your* motivations. You can even copy and paste these questions and to send to potential recruiters. You will easily be able to discern who knows their stuff and who is full of it.

Lastly, a great recruiter will *consult*. They will give you objective feedback even if it means risking their commission. They will be the difference between you getting the job and never even getting a response from HR.

If you can't find a recruiter, that's ok, as this eBook aims to guide you through the process even if you don't have the assistance of a recruiter!

CHAPTER 5:

THE INTERVIEW PROCESS

"If you're not stubborn, you'll give up on experiments too soon. And if you're not flexible, you'll pound your head against the wall, and you won't see a different solution to a problem you're trying to solve."

-Jeff Bezos

* * * * *

The Amazon interview process can be grueling. However, the good news is that it's fairly consistent. Because we know the structure of the interview beforehand, it makes it much easier to prepare and minimizes surprises. It doesn't mean the interview is easy (not by a long shot!), but it does mean that you will not be going in blind.

Here's the basic process:

Step #1: Screening call with HR or internal recruiter

This lasts about 45 minutes to 1 hour. HR or the recruiter will spend most of the time asking questions about your career. They will usually start in chronological order from your first job to your most recent position. You're expected to answer questions in the STAR format (more on this below).

It's unlikely you'll get too much feedback during that conversation, and it might seem more "informational" or casual -- but it hardly ever is. Job-seekers tend to come out of the conversation feeling good, which is strange because you have no indication of whether or not you made it to the next round! I believe the reason for this is because the recruiter/HR will let people talk most of the time without interrupting them. People love to talk but don't realize whether or not they're saying the *right* things. Here's the best way to approach this initial call and to make sure you *are* saying right things:

Practice talking about your career from start to finish. There will inevitably be pieces you've forgotten, including the reasons you've left certain jobs and so forth. The reasons for our decisions often get lost in the fog of time, so you might need to review and brainstorm. Typically, the past five years of your career are considered the most relevant.

Go deep. You will likely be asked about your biggest failure and biggest achievement in your career. Choose your examples wisely. It's better to have one or two very detailed and pertinent examples (in the past five years), rather than ten shallow answers.

Don't talk too much. We have a tendency to be overly descriptive with our answers, but it's usually best to keep concise. I recommend keeping each answer to one minute or less. If the interviewer wants more details, they will probe.

Step #2: Interview with hiring manager

This portion is either in person or via a phone call with the hiring manager, who would be your direct manager. The hiring manager is on your side. They have the biggest pain point, meaning that they *really* need to hire someone. It's in their best interest to be nice to you, and they usually are. That doesn't mean you won't get tough questions. However, I find that this first meeting with the hiring manager is going to be one of the main chances where you get to ask specific questions about the position.

For this interview, you should be ready to sell yourself. Prepare fewer questions about the company culture, and more questions about what kind of goals the manager has, what projects you would work on immediately, and their expectations for the position.

The hiring manager will usually be the "easiest" interviewer you come in contact with. Your conversation will likely be about the position itself and your career goals. You should use this meeting as a chance to learn as much as possible about the job. You want to figure out: *What would I be doing on a daily basis and what will it be like working with this manager?*

Step #3: Writing Test

For certain positions, you will be required to submit a writing test, which will be roughly two pages and given to you to complete on your own so that you can do it at home. The best way to write this is using the STAR format, which I will explain in the section below. My recommendations are to:

1. Keep the length to two or three pages - no more than that.
2. Revise your writing sample to be as logical and concise as possible.
3. Always include the reasoning behind decisions you made in the story.
4. Include numbers/data where you can.

This writing sample is taken seriously as part of the interview process because as an Amazon employee you will not be using

PowerPoint presentations. In fact, PowerPoint presentations are not allowed at Amazon. Instead, you have to write reports frequently and explain your thoughts in a detailed written format.

This is a two-page essay to be written at home about a topic of the hiring manager's choice. You are typically given a week to complete it. Depending on the level and position, this step may not be required.

Step #4: Final "Loop" Interview

This is anywhere from two to nine interviews you will have, usually in succession. The number of interviewers correlates with the level of the position. So, a Level 7 (L7) position would have seven total interviewers; an L5 would have five, and so on.

The remainder of the loop interviewers will be a grab bag. Some interviewers will be related to your position and others will be from a completely different department. In fact, it is likely you will not even work with most of them in your actual job, or they might not know what job you are interviewing for. They are simply involved in the hiring process to test your culture fit.

The loop interview process also includes someone called a "bar raiser" who tends to be a more senior interviewer. They are there to literally raise the hiring bar. You will not be informed who they are, but they are not in your department and tend to have at least 3+ years at the Company with a strong track record of hiring and retaining employees. There is nothing extra you can do to prepare for this meeting. However, this interviewer will typically be more difficult, because they have more interview experience. Knowing this, I recommend that you are *mentally* prepared to focus for a 1-hour conversation that could be intense. If you are feeling tired, then it is probably best to reschedule the interview for a time when you are feeling 100% alert and focused.

All of the loop interviewers are there to provide a more objective assessment, and at the end of the day they are looking one thing: **your fit with the leadership principles.** Or in other words, your fit within Amazon culture.

Step #5: Hiring Meeting

After you finish meeting with all of the interviewers, the people you met with will convene in one room together to debate whether they should hire you or not. Usually, you will know the result within one week of finishing final interviews. There's not much you can do at this stage, but if you haven't already, definitely send a thank you note to the people you have met. Sit tight!

Step #6: Offer Meeting

If all is positive, HR will ask for your current and expected salary. Based on this information and the level of the job, they will send you a written offer. Sometimes, HR will invite the interviewee to their office to explain this in person in an "offer meeting" instead of a phone call. This meeting isn't a place where you will negotiate. Any negotiation should come before the offer meeting.

Step #7: Reference Check.

If your position is above L5, Amazon usually requires one or two reference checks, sometimes more for senior roles. These are conducted by the HR manager or hiring manager over the phone and last about 15-20 minutes. Typically they will request at least one former boss and one former peer, or if you are in a management role, they will want to speak one of your former direct reports.

How long does the process take?

I have seen this entire process, beginning with sending an application to getting an offer, take anywhere from three weeks to three months. Usually the more senior the position, the longer the process takes, due to the number of interviews to schedule. After the loop interview, everyone that you met in the process has to convene in one room and debate your candidacy. This is referred to as the hiring meeting. Once they decide, they will be able to give you either a verbal offer or give you feedback on why it didn't work out.

Depending on everyone's schedule this can take a while to book. Typically the hiring meeting is scheduled within a week, however for more senior positions, it takes longer, since it is challenging to get VPs and directors in the same room at the same time.

Also, there are situations where interviewers can't come to an agreement in the hiring meeting and the vote is split. In that case, they may have to meet again, or they may invite you in for another interview, a "final, final" interview.

You can reach out to the internal or external recruiter and simply ask them, *"When is the date of the hiring meeting?"* Once you receive the date and time they will be having the hiring meeting, 99% of the time if you don't hear back from them on that day it means you didn't get the job. Unfortunately, it can take them a while to give you the negative feedback. If the feedback is positive, however, they'll be eager to contact you on that day to tell you the good news.

The process can vary depending on a host of factors, such as the level of the position. For example, if the hiring manager is too busy all week for an interview, then sometimes HR will schedule the interview with a different stakeholder. I have even seen hiring managers meet people twice as part of the loop.

If your position requires lots of data analysis or use of Excel, then you can expect to have a 20-30 minute test included somewhere in the interview process. This test is not communicated ahead of time, but it typically comes in the beginning stages of your interviews, before the loop.

Engineering and Technical Interviews

The leadership principles and your culture fit are critical to getting hired, but the greater your technical expertise, the more flexibility Amazon will have on the 'culture' piece.

Amazon will give you either a surprise test during the interview or an actual engineering/ coding test (with advance notice). If you are applying for any position that requires the use of Excel (it will say on the job description), they'll probably test your pivot table skills for 20-30 minutes as part of the interview process. Be prepared.

If you are applying for a business analyst position, for example, they probably won't tell you if there is a test, but depending on how technical it is you can at least expect they will test your SQL skills in the interview. This may not necessarily require you to use any database management system, but will come in the form of a question like, *"If you have two SQL database tables that are not joined together, how would you create another table to join them?"*

For any positions that require programming skills, you can expect the coding test to come **at the start of the process**. This means it will either be your first or second interview, right after speaking to an HR person/recruiter. This is not going to be an extremely complex test that will require hours of your time. It covers the fundamentals of the language so you should brush up on the basics. You can use a service like Gainlo to work through mock interviews.

Keep in mind there is no rush to get through all of the interviews. If you feel you need 2-3 weeks to brush up on certain skills, or can't answer some of the questions above, then make sure you practice ahead of time before applying for the job. If you have already applied and feel overwhelmed, and not ready to answer, then request to postpone the meetings.

With that in mind, here are some tips for the technical interviews.

1. Always bring a pen, a backup pen, and paper even though it's a 'programming interview'.
2. Don't be afraid to restate the question/problem. You might have some time limit (an hour), but it makes sense to make sure you fully understand the question, then figure out the best method to solve, and lastly spend a fraction of the time actually executing.
3. Understand the properties of data structures and how to use them.
4. Understand how your language uses internal structures to manage the codes/objects you write.
5. Like all Amazon interviews, being concise is key. This means not talking too much, but not leaving out key points. The interview should never be a monologue.

Your technical skills are an important part of the hiring equation, but it's also important for interviewers to know what you did, how you did it, and in what context. Using the STAR Method is the best way to to do this (See Chapter 7). Specifically, Amazon hiring managers want to know a few things about your technical expertise. Be ready to address these two big questions.

1. *How you work on a team.* Are you a strong communicator? Have you worked cross- functionally? What examples do you have of this?
2. *Achievements + impact.* You might have created some great system, but how was this used? What impact did it have in the business? Can you speak in terms of speed, efficiency, ROI, sales, revenue, marketing, etc.?

Furthermore, there are hundreds of questions that have already been posted online for you to practice.

1. **Amazon.com Software Development Engineer I Interview Questions:** https://bit.ly/2Dsku0K
2. **Amazon.com Intern Interview Questions:** https://bit.ly/2yWoe6J
3. **Amazon Interview questions for Engineers:** https://bit.ly/2ySyjS0
4. **Amazon.com Software Development Engineer Intern Interview Questions:** https://bit.ly/2ASgkwo

Lastly, I recommend reading the book Cracking the Coding Interview which will give you a more thorough list of questions to study!

CHAPTER 6:

THE LEADERSHIP PRINCIPLES

"The principles are embodied in the natural way of thought and the common language spoken on a day-to-day basis by Amazonians regardless of function, domain, role, level, business model or target market."

—Arun Prasath, Principal Engineer at Amazon

After speaking to dozens of hiring managers at all levels, including VPs and directors, the number one piece of advice for interviewing at Amazon was consistent across the board: **know the leadership principles like the back of your hand.**

You should be living and breathing the leadership principles before interviewing at Amazon.

The leadership principles are a <u>list of 14 values</u> that define and shape the Company culture. Amazonians use them daily in all levels of decision making. These principles are not just some inspirational wall-hanging that you see at some companies. *Being familiar with these principles is the most important part of the interview process.*

But it is not enough *to know* the leadership principles; you also have to *understand* them conceptually *along with specific examples from your background.* Preparing for this will likely make up the bulk of your preparation. **You should have one example ready for each principle**. Successful interviewees usually spend five to six hours minimum preparing.

I will explain each principle in detail before sharing real Amazon interview questions connected to each one.

#1: Customer Obsession

"Leaders start with the customer and work backwards. They work vigorously to earn and keep customer trust. Although leaders pay attention to competitors, they obsess over customers."

Amazon has been described as the world's most customer-centric business, and this principle is testament to that. Most companies are competition-focused and want to make sure they do not fall behind. Amazon, on the other hand, looks at their entire business through the eyes of the customer.

Here are a few examples of customer obsession that happen internally:

1. Amazon runs usability tests on all their categories online to make sure the platform is consistent with the customer's needs.
2. *When faced with a difficult product or engineering decision, Amazonians ask the question, "how would the customer respond?"*
3. The best customer service means the customer does not need to call Amazon. In other words, issues are solved before they arise and if they do arise, they are resolved quickly.

Jeff Bezos frequently brings an empty chair to executive meetings as a reminder that there is always someone else in the room - the customer. Here is a list of a few more ways customer obsession manifests internally https://www.salesforce.com/blog/2013/06/jeff-bezos-lessons.html.

Review this slide deck by Kintan B https://bit.ly/2F6YOss who is a product management director at Amazon. He gives his definition of customer obsession and what it means for his team.

Real questions asked in the interview:

What is the difference between customer focus and customer obsession? How do you pursue real customer feedback, not just solicit for compliments? How have you WOW'd your customers in the past?

Share an example where you use customer feedback to drive an improvement in your previous business.

When do you think it's reasonable and appropriate to push back on a very difficult customer? How have you used data to better understand your customers/clients?

#2: Ownership

"Leaders are owners. They think long term and do not sacrifice long-term value for short- term results. They act on behalf of the entire company, beyond their own team. They never say 'that's not my job.' Drive the business like your own car, not some cheap weekend rental."

Working at Amazon often requires you to go beyond the scope of your job description to get the job done. This means acting quickly, gathering resources, and wearing many different hats. That could be anything from simply mean picking up a piece of trash on the floor, to performing sales activities even though you are in a marketing job. Not every day, but you have to be willing to stretch outside the box.

Similarly, when you fail in a project, taking full responsibility and ownership for that failure is expected. Ownership is synonymous with accountability.

Real questions:

When did you go outside of the boundaries of your defined role to fix a problem? Describe a time when you have taken ownership in your job.

How do you balance focusing on your day to day tasks without losing track of the long term vision?

#3: Invent and Simplify

Leaders expect and require innovation and invention from their teams and always find ways to simplify. They are externally aware, look for new ideas from everywhere, and are not limited by "not invented here." As we do new things, we accept that we may be misunderstood for long periods of time.

Scaling a business that can be used not by just a few thousand people, but by millions of consumers is always a consideration. Amazonians are always thinking about how to make things smoother, faster, cheaper and better for the customer. Often times this takes the form of "kaizen" or continuous process improvement and automation.

Real questions:

What is the most innovative or inventive thing you've achieved (process improvement, product idea)?

When was the last time you tried something new?

#4: Are Right, A Lot

Leaders have strong business judgment and good instincts. They seek diverse perspectives and work to disconfirm their beliefs.

Ultimately, your interview comes down to results. Be prepared to discuss the impact you have had in your previous job (in tangible terms) and the business knowledge you have gained over the years. After all, they are expecting you to succeed.

That said, showing humility is expected. If you speak only of your achievements and no mistakes or failures, this is a big red flag for Amazon. They want to know you have experienced a range of failures and successes, which have shaped you as a person and as a leader.

Real questions:

What is your biggest achievement?

What tangible impact did your achievement have?

#5: Hire and Develop the Best

Leaders raise the performance bar with every hire and promotion. They recognize exceptional talent and willingly move them throughout the organization. Leaders develop leaders and take seriously their role in coaching others. We work on behalf of our people to invent mechanisms for development like Career Choice.

They want to know your management style and how you have developed people in the past – did they get promoted and what did they achieve? What did you learn from the experiences? Even if you have no management experience or are not interviewing for a management role, you could discuss how you help others around you, how you have trained people, or how helped new starters in your previous company.

Real questions:

Who was your best hire and why?

What was your biggest hiring mistake? What did you learn from it? How do you earn trust from new employees?

What is your management philosophy?

#6: Insist on the Highest Standards

Leaders have relentlessly high standards—many people may think these standards are unreasonably high. Leaders are continually raising the bar and driving their teams to deliver high-quality products, services, and processes. Leaders ensure that defects do not get sent down the line and that problems are fixed, so they stay fixed.

This principle relates to everything from your attention to detail to the small things (what a customer things about the color of a button), all the way to hiring the right people. Never compromise on this.

Real question:

How have you raised the bar to increase quality of your work?

#7: Think Big

Thinking small is a self-fulfilling prophecy. Leaders create and communicate a bold direction that inspires results. They think differently and look around corners for ways to serve customers.

This brings up the dichotomy of strategy vs. tactics. Strategy means a longer-term planning of a goal, like a yearly revenue target. The tactics mean the tasks and methods you use to achieve the goal, like the specific clients you will approach and sales techniques you will use. "Think big" means that you come up with the strategy and vision.

You do not have to be a "leader" of people to apply this principle. I find there are usually two skills that are mentioned together: dive deep vs. think big. People who have been in a deeply analytical position might not always see the bigger picture. On the other hand, people that are always looking months or years ahead may not focus on the detail. You need to be able to strike a balance between the two, at least in the eyes of the interviewer.

Real questions:

Sometimes we can get buried in the details and lose sight of the big picture. How do you ensure this doesn't happen?

#8: Bias for Action

Speed matters in business. Many decisions and actions are reversible and do not need extensive study. We value calculated risk taking.

Often, people get caught up in "analysis paralysis," meaning that they spend too much time planning and do not take action quickly enough. Amazon believes you do not always need to be 100% sure to make a decision. When you are 80% certain and have a strong business judgment, it is better to decide now with limited information rather than wait another nine months.

Real questions:

Describe a time where you made a judgment call with limited information. How do you overcome analysis paralysis?

What is your level of risk tolerance? Why? How does this manifest itself in your work?

#9: Frugality

Accomplish more with less. Constraints breed resourcefulness, self-sufficiency, and invention. There are no extra points for growing headcount, budget size, or fixed expense.

Amazon does not have a "country club" culture. They operate like a big startup. Money goes towards improving the customer experience and not throwing money around on non- essentials. Rather, analyzing the best options and spending the money wisely.

Amazon employees notoriously do not get cell phones or generous expense accounts — the Company saves a lot of money on unnecessary perks.

Real question:

Describe a time when you improved a process with limited budget.

#10: Learn and Be Curious

Leaders are never done learning and always seek to improve themselves. They are curious about new possibilities and act to explore them.

Curiosity leads to creativity. This leads to new ideas, innovation, and frugality. Amazon wants to know how you come up with these ideas - whether that's staying up to date with trends or blending other disciplines to create something.

Real question:

How do you find the time to stay inspired, acquire new knowledge, and innovate in your work?

#11 Earn Trust.

Leaders listen attentively, speak candidly, and treat others respectfully. They are vocally self-critical, even when doing so is awkward or embarrassing. Leaders do not believe their or their team's body odor smells of perfume. They benchmark themselves and their teams against the best.

Amazon wants to see how you have been proactive in revealing problems and mistakes. The first step in fixing a problem is admitting it exists. Then open your kimono, figuratively speaking, and take responsibility for your action. This is where humility comes in and remembering not to boast about your achievements.

Real question #1: *Share an example of a failure in your career.*

Real question #2: *How do you earn trust from a team that you inherited?*

#12: Dive Deep

Leaders operate at all levels, stay connected to the details, audit frequently, and are skeptical when metrics and anecdote differ. No task is beneath them.

People struggle with this principle the most. Interviewers will ask you "why, why, why" as a follow up to your answers to get more details. You have to be ready to talk about what YOU did specifically in the situation, and how that affected the business. They do not want to know what others did; rather, they are more interested in your specific accomplishments. Use the pronoun "I" instead of "we" and it will make a big difference to the interviewer.

They are expecting a granular level of detail — i.e., how big the marketing budget was, what your analysis was, WHY you chose that train of thought, how you allocated the budget, what marketing methods YOU used, the metrics and financial impact of that.

Real questions:

Describe a problem you solved recently. Why did it happen, what was the root cause of the problem?

Why did you change your last job?

Walk me through your biggest failure. What could you have done differently?

If you have a team, can you describe what their daily activities are? How do you measure them?

#13: Have Backbone; Disagree and Commit.

Leaders are obligated to respectfully challenge decisions when they disagree, even when doing so is uncomfortable or exhausting. Leaders have conviction and are tenacious. They do not compromise for the sake of social cohesion. Once a decision is determined, they commit wholly.

Disagreement is encouraged as long as you have data and a logical point to your disagreement. Think of examples of when you have challenged the status quo.

Real question:

Give an example when you had to push back to HQ or challenged a decision in your organization.

23 More Real Questions from Amazon Interviews

1. Tell the story of the last time you had to apologize to someone.

2. A customer tries to convince you that a crow is white. (crows are black). What do you tell him?

3. How would you improve Amazon's website?

4. You have 30 people working under you with 2 working indirect. Each employee can do 150 units/hour. Each work day has two 15 min breaks and one 30 min lunch. In a 5 day work week, how many total units can you complete?

5. What is the most difficult situation you have ever faced in your life? How did you handle it?

6. How would you tell a customer what Wi-Fi is?

7. Should we sell private label cleaning products?

8. Which Amazon leadership principle do you resonate most with?

9. How do you calculate lifetime customer value?

10. What would be the sample class design for a tic tac toe game? (question for developers)

11. What makes you uncomfortable?

12. Talk about a time when you had to fire someone or make a very unpopular decision.

13. Design a card game.

14. What is your favorite service?

15. What is the difference between customer service and customer obsession?

16. Give me an example of a time when you did not meet a client's expectation. What happened, and how did you attempt to rectify the situation?

17. Tell me about a time you needed to get information from someone who wasn't very responsive. What did you do?

18. Tell me about a time when you had to leave a task unfinished

19. Tell me about a time when you mentored someone.

20. When you're working with a large number of customers, it's tricky to deliver excellent service to them all. How do you go about prioritizing your customers' needs?

21. Give me two examples of when you did more than what was required in any job experience.

22. Give me an example of a time when you were 75% of the way through a project, and you had to pivot strategy– how were you able to make that into a success story?

23. If your direct manager was instructing you to do something you disagreed with, how would you handle it?

#14: Deliver Results

Leaders focus on the key inputs for their business and deliver them with the right quality and in a timely fashion. Despite setbacks, they rise to the occasion and never settle.

At the end of the day, it is all about performance and results. Whether that is a financial impact, improving something within the business, or launching a product, you have to show how you made an impact.

Real questions:

What is your biggest accomplishment? What impact did you make in your previous company? How do you balance humility with strong leadership?

* * * * *

As you have probably noticed, a lot of the leadership principles have significant overlap. "Deliver results" and "are right a lot" are similar. "Invent and simplify" and "frugality" are connected. The principle of "dive deep" can be shown by the *way* you answer your questions. In other words, you can "dive deep" by being very detailed in your storytelling when describing your past achievements. This is good news because it means that you can find one example that will encompass several principles.

For example, if you are asked to "Describe a problem you solved recently," you could share a story about a new customer that you acquired. The story could include details of how you had to "earn trust" from your client, brainstorm new ideas in a different industry ("learn and be curious"), and ultimately how you "delivered results."

This means that you only need to prepare four or five detailed examples of your previous achievements. You can use these examples to answer most questions that Amazon will throw at you. As long as they are related to the leadership principles, you can rest assured that they will be seen as relevant.

CHAPTER 7:

THE STAR METHOD

Amazon largely uses **behavioral interview** questions to assess your background. This means that they believe your past performance will predict future performance.

In most of the interviews, you will be doing the talking and explaining your background. The interviewers will do little talking, except for five to ten minutes of Q&A at the end. This means you will discuss your achievements, failures, improvements, previous job responsibilities, and break down the logic behind your decisions.

The Amazon recruiter will ask your behavioral interview questions to determine if you fit the principles. Interviewers have a checkbox for each of the principles they are testing, and usually, each interviewer is responsible for one or two principles.

You should be ready to answer all of the questions that I mentioned above in the leadership principle section. The best way to do this is using the STAR method, which Amazon even recommends.

STAR stands for:

- Situation
- Task

- Action
- Result

1. What was the problem? Like any good story, you will need to start by painting a picture of what happened, where you were, and the people involved. This is the *situation*.

2. What was your responsibility? You have to identify what this is and describe it clearly. This is the *task*.

3. Once you have decided the goal or outcome you would like to achieve, you need to take steps to get there. What steps did you take and why did you take them? That is the *action*.

4. After moving forward with your plan, what happened? Were you successful, and what did you learn? This is the *result*.

It is as simple as that. I suggest writing down every single leadership principle and coming up with an example of how you have demonstrated that specific principle. Structure your notes in the STAR format so your responses will naturally follow the structure.

It is important to note that past performance does not mean that you have done the same job in the past. Even if you are a recent graduate with zero work experience or are switching industries midway through your career, companies can assess your past performance. But how?

Cheri Huber, Zen Buddhist meditation teacher and author sums it up nicely when she said, *"How you do anything is how you do everything."* When you describe your leadership role on the tennis team in university, this reflects your leadership ability. When you organized a large event for a political campaign as an intern, this shows your organizational ability. When you worked three part-time jobs to fund your education, this shows your grit and work ethic. When you broke the sales record in your previous company, this shows that you know a thing or two about sales.

All of these examples and more can be told as a story using the STAR Method. Companies have certain job requirements in mind when assessing job seekers. However, they use these requirements (usually written in a job description) as more of a guideline. That is why you should not get hung up on every single detail of Amazon's job description.

Thus the importance of being able to tell a story about what you might be doing on the job is one of the best ways that you are going to be able to show them you are capable. Of course, you might have a specific experience or achievement written on your resume that indicates, "Yes, I've done this before." However, it is unlikely that all of the details are spelled out on your resume, so greater *context* is necessary in order to explain the relevance. This is where your storytelling powers comes in.

With a good story, you will be able to answer questions such as, "Tell me about a time when you had to show leadership" or "what was your biggest achievement?" You will be able to answer any of the leadership principle example-questions that I stated above.

I realize that it is impossible to remember 100 different stories in the Amazon interview. Instead, you should pick four or five key stories that you can reuse. It is more important to be able to logically explain your story and provide a greater amount of detail, than having a lot of surface-level answers.

I have written an entire book on how to use the STAR Method, which you can find here if you are interested in diving deeper. http://starinterviewmethod.com/

CHAPTER 8:

QUESTIONS THAT YOU SHOULD ASK THE INTERVIEWER

Asking good questions is crucial at every step of the interview process. I have seen people get rejected after their interviews for failing to show curiosity and ask good, business-minded questions.

It is likely that you will have questions pop into your head during the interview, in which case you should take a mental note, ask immediately, or write them down in a notepad. I would recommend preparing at least 10-15 questions for the hiring manager because they are the window into the job itself.

We can break down potential questions into a few categories. I've provided some standard questions that will open up a conversation for you with Amazon, but you will need to prepare your own questions depending on the position and your individual curiosities.

The Position

- What are the three most important leadership principles for this job?
- How do you define success for this position? What metrics are you using to measure my accomplishments?
- What specific tools will I be using on the job?

- What is a typical day like?
- What are the opportunities for advancement and growth in this position?
- Do you have any hesitations about my skills or experience for this job?
- Is this a new or replacement position? If it's a replacement, why did the previous person leave?

The Business

- How does this service/product fit into the greater picture?
- How do you measure customer service?
- What important initiatives are you working on for the next 6-12 months?
- How does this role contribute to larger company goals?

The Team

- How would you describe the team culture?
- Can you tell me about members of the team?
- What are the team's strengths and weaknesses?
- What have been the biggest challenges this year for the team?

The Interviewer

- Why did you decide to join Amazon?
- What is your management style and philosophy?
- What is your expectation of me for the first 90 days of the job?
- How do you deliver negative feedback?
- What are your favorite and least favorite things about working here?

* * * * *

Managers don't like it when you ask them the question "why is this position open?" because they don't see it as a relevant question to succeeding in the job. That said, it's important for you to ask the question.

From their perspective, this falls under "HR question" like "How many vacation days do I get?" and "How many people are there in the company?" The hiring manager would rather focus on the future — how you're going to help them, what skills you're going to bring and what problems you're going to solve.

But if they get defensive or nervous then that's your yellow flag. There are lots of situations where you could be set up for failure and don't know it until you're actually in the job.

For example, if there's someone on the team that undermines other people, and people are leaving because of that person, this may not even be evident to the manager! Ideally, you want to ask the recruiter and HR as they're going to be less sensitive, from my experience.

Lastly, a better way to phrase the question more softly would be, *"I'm curious about the history of this job opening — is the job open because of the growth of the team and additional headcount, or some other reason?"*

* * * * *

The biggest red flag for a company is if you ask questions that are not business minded. When you ask something like "what are the vacation allotments and time off?" and "how soon can I start?!" they might answer politely, but inside they are wondering why you chose to ask such a question.

Why? Because those are not "business-minded" questions and they are not going to help the company in any way. Don't worry; you can still ask those questions to HR later. But don't ask the hiring manager.

Over the past few years in recruitment, I've found one thing that really set apart the typical questions asked by most interviewees vs. the superstar questions.

The short answer: *commercialism.*

Long Answer: The idea of being "commercial" means that you fundamentally understand how a business works. You understand how it makes money, what the levers of the business are, and can make good judgments based on that. It doesn't matter what your profession is.

The money ain't growing on trees.

It's understanding the why and the gears in the machine. You can go for months and years working at a company but not really understand how it operates. Commercialism is something that might come naturally to some people — they can smell the money, or they are problem solvers. They need to understand how something works. But for most people commercialism will come with time. It will be facilitated by having worked with a strong manager/leader and taking a proactive approach to constantly improving themselves.

Commercialism includes all of the following:

1. An understanding of the end product your business is selling
2. Understanding how the company makes money and the costs associated with that
3. Knowing who the customers are
4. An interest in business and an understanding of the wider environment in which the business operates in
5. Understanding what category the business fits in, the overall market, and market trends

Knowing this, we can come up with some great and detailed questions. If you don't have all of the answers to the five questions above for the company you are interviewing for, then you can start to dive deep.

For example, you could ask the following.

Who are your biggest customers in terms of revenue? What is your customer retention rate? What are your customers like and how do you communicate with them? How much time do you spend with them?

How do you measure customer service?

How is performance measured in the company and in this position? What specific KPI's (key performance indicators) do you use and are they weekly, monthly, quarterly, biannual, yearly, etc.?

What is the three-year growth plan? What do you think will be the biggest challenge around this and what specific initiatives and tactics are being implemented to achieve these goals?

What CRM system do you use to track information? What is your management style/philosophy?

What is the approval process for making decisions in the company (related to product, sales, marketing etc.)?

What is your business model? Is your business cyclical? What are your biggest revenue streams? Do you see the business model changing?

What are the biggest weaknesses in your business and what are you doing to address them?

Once you ask some of these questions, you'll likely get *a lot* of information from the interviewer.

They'll likely be impressed that you're getting into the level of granularity. It shows that you have a genuine interest in how the business works and their goals.

You can then ask follow up questions, of course. And you have the massive benefit of now understanding the inner-workings of the business.

Companies are going to hire you for 1 of 2 reasons, or both:

1. You can make the company money
2. You can save the company money

Keep that in mind when you are asking questions, and it'll be easier to focus relevant questions. Never be afraid to sound "dumb" because they will ultimately appreciate your inquisitiveness!

CHAPTER 9:

THE PHILOSOPHY OF IMPACT

Companies hire you because they think you have skills to do a job. Clients want to work with you because they think you have something to add to their business. You face competition from millions of other people around the world. People in India that you've never met. And machines. If your job requires a repetitive task then it is likely to be automated by an algorithm in the near future.

Now more than ever you are faced with a very important question: *What value are you adding?*

It might seem painfully cliché or overused. It is. But it's important. Amazon hiring managers want to understand what you're going to do for their business.

Fortunately, it's very simple. Companies just want to know how you are going to help them. It comes down to two things.

1. Can you make the company money?
2. Can you save the company money?

Really, that's it.

Often if you are in a job you have tasks and are performing actions that ultimately add to the growth of a company. If you can understand and articulate how you did this, then it means that you have a commercial understanding of the business. And while some companies truly love to see people grow and flourish, and make a fun environment that provides meaningful work — people are ultimately expendable. People are ultimately expendable to them *unless* they are solving a problem. The more valuable you are, the less expendable you are.

That's linked to making or saving money. *That* is how they define value.

If you are a CFO, you could be saving the company millions through your corporate structuring and astute tax savings methods. If you are a great salesperson, you could be making the company millions in revenue and fueling the growth.

This is money the company can use to hire more people and build more stuff.

You might understand this conceptually, but the biggest challenge for many people is linking their tasks and actions to a monetary result.

Often they aren't given that information or are not incentivized to think about it — at least not until they are in more senior or in entrepreneurial roles. Even if "money" is not part of your specific result, it could very well be part of the impact. Quantify it.

Let's take an example:

John is doing data entry as an executive assistant for the CEO of a Fortune 500 company. He writes up reports, does online research, and books meetings for the CEO. In an interview with

a potential employer, John gives a STAR story and describes how he created a more efficient schedule and task management system for the CEO.

But he doesn't stop there.

With the new task management and scheduling system I developed for the CEO, I was able to save him a significant amount of time and added an extra 4 hours per week to his calendar.

While this number may not seem large at first, this has freed up his time to be more involved in hands-on strategy across different departments. Within three months of introducing the new system, the CEO was able to focus his effort on a new product launch that was behind schedule, which ultimately launched on time and became one of our top selling products for the year.

John was able to free up time for the CEO, whose time is extremely valuable. We know that his time is valuable, but John makes a point to explicitly state *how* valuable it was. There was a big product launch and the free time allowed for him to work on this, which he did, and then launched in on time.

The company is selling stuff and making money. John's hard work has helped the company make money by saving the CEO time.

We can see that it's a pretty powerful *result* from John.

Now, be careful not to take a huge leap without substantiation. It would be a stretch for John to say *"I'd like to think that my scheduling system resulted in millions of dollars' worth of revenue for the company."*

Correlation doesn't equal causation.

This sounds a bit like an inflated ego, and while it's good to take ownership of your work unless you have hard proof, it's best not to take it *that* far. Maybe the CEO would have found time to do it anyways...he probably would have.

The greater point is that John can attach meaning to what he did. Why it was important and the impact it had.

He didn't just "make a system and save time," but he did it and could articulate what the CEO was doing with that time, which was ultimately beneficial for the company.

So, the million dollar question is, how are *you* saving/making your company money?

CHAPTER 10:

COMMON PITFALLS

Failure stories. Amazon will almost certainly ask you to describe a time when you failed in your career or life. Many people make the mistake of trying to spin the example as something that turned out very positive in the end. This is likely because it can hurt to talk about our failures and we want to make a good impression. However, Amazon actually *wants* to hear your failure stories. They are expecting something substantial and impactful that. It should be something that was etched in your memory and *hurt.*

For example, when asked about your failure story, a poor story would be "the time you didn't efficiently use the marketing budget and wasted money." This would **not** be a good example because the marketing budget is already set. This failure did not cause much damage.

A better story would be the time you hired someone and realized they were a terrible fit for your culture, and subsequently fired them after five months. In the process, you wasted thousands of dollars, sucked time from managers, and hurt company morale. That is a painful and tangible example. You can, of course, still talk about what you learned from the experience, Amazon wants to see that you learned through the failure.

A good, juicy failure story needs to have a real negative impact on others. If you did something wrong in your previous position but faced no consequences, then it is probably not sufficient. When you lose a client and your team suffers — that is bad. When you fail to meet a deadline and a project is canceled, that reflects poorly on you *and* the company.

In the end, this ties back to the leadership principle of taking *ownership.* Make sure to prepare two examples of failures and do not be afraid to speak transparently about your mistakes.

Dive Deep. The reason Amazon interviewers dig so deep into the details of your past is to make sure that you actually did what you said you did. The logic is that the best way to discover your true role and responsibility in a job is to grill you on the details. If you said that you were a "sales leader," they want to know the story of how you closed the biggest sales deal. Was your boss in the meeting with you? Did someone else do the contract negotiation? Or were you involved in every step of the negotiation on your own? The depth and scope of your responsibility will come to light through this storytelling.

People who prepare the least for interviews tend to break down when "dive deep" is tested. They get flustered because they are asked to justify their thinking and decision-making process. Frequently, Amazon interviewers will ask you, "Why did you decide to take that action? How did you analyze your options? Why did you not push back to your supervisor to try a different option?" You need to be able to explain the logic behind all of your examples.

Diving deep can also be required in the form of *tangible outcomes.* When you describe the size of your marketing budget, they want a number. When you talk about the ROI they also want to know that number. You can talk about your great sales achievement and share a number, but how does that compare to others in the company? How does your sales number compare to the target this year and also last year? Providing context and specific details to describe the impact you made is key.

When you prepare 30 different examples from your previous work, it is unlikely that you are going to remember all of the details and reasons for your decision making. Thus the best way to prepare is to limit the number of examples you prepare to five or six key stories in your career. This way, you will be able to dive deep every time.

Not Answering a Question. One of the biggest mistakes I see people make is when they cop out of answering questions. When you say "I don't know" or "next question please," then you will likely be disqualified immediately. I realize this sounds unfair at first and you might be thinking, *"How am I expected to know all of the answers?"*

This does not mean you have to have a perfect answer to every question. That is an impossible expectation, and interviewers realize everyone might answer differently. Rather, they are more interested in your thinking *process.* They want to know how you break down a problem and how you go about solving it, even if the answer is incorrect. Furthermore, Amazon expects interviewees to think on their feet.

If you need time to think about an answer, then you can simply ask the interviewer to give you one minute to think about it. There is nothing wrong with some silence as you contemplate. Also, you can always request to come back to the question later. Write it down so you do not forget. Whatever you do, the point is to make sure that you always provide some sort of answer!

Long Winded Answers. You will always have more to say than you actually need to. Let that one sink in for a second.

It's important that your answers are never more than a couple of minutes long. If they are, you will be seen as verbose, and it will be marked heavily against you. The challenge is that the interviewer is not going to give you any indication if they want you to stop talking. They will patiently sit there and listen to you while you dig your own grave.

This may sound a little bit harsh, but it's one of the most common traps. People tend to get nervous and ramble, which happens to all of us. To stop yourself from doing this, always use the STAR approach. Second, use a mental timer to keep your answer short and concise. If the interviewer wants more details, they will ask for more. Rather than assume what the interviewer wants to hear, give the concise version of what you're trying to say, and let them probe deeper if they are interested.

Negative Attitude. A top executive recruiter at Amazon told me about the two types of interviewees that she has encountered over the years. She has interviewed thousands of people and hired many. There are many personalities, strengths, weaknesses, and so forth. Throughout these interviews, she has noticed that people typically fall into two categories, which ultimately determine their success in the interview process.

> **Type #1:** This person sees themselves as the victim. The interviewer cannot be trusted because they are trying to weed people out of the interview process or might lowball them on a job offer. They proceed cautiously. They are not open to feedback and do not accept the fact that interview preparation will take hours and is not something they are going to be naturally good at. They might be a good

storyteller, but that does not mean they are telling the right stories. This person might have a lot of years of great work experience which allows them to believe that they are naturally good at interviewing. They are then surprised when they do not get the call back for the second interview.

Type #2: This person knows that they do not know everything. They may or may not have a strong understanding of their own background. They may or may not be confident in how they express themselves. But they are open to learning about an individual company's interview process and can take constructive feedback from recruiters and hiring managers. They are always prepared. They realize that no matter how much job experience they have, that does not make them naturally great interviewees. They spend hours and hours preparing for interviews and are constantly learning. They are the ones who get the job despite not being the loudest in the room.

The point is that it does not matter how much experience you have. It does not matter if you, yourself, have interviewed hundreds of people. You are on the other side of the table now. In fact, those who have a lot of experience interviewing others inevitably get set to a certain "style" of interviewing that may not be relevant.

Good interviewees must hone their approach, remain adaptable, and spend ample time preparing using the leadership principles.

Which type of job seeker are *you*?

CHAPTER 11:

CHANCES OF
RECEIVING AN OFFER

I asked an HR executive at Amazon how many people they had to interview to hire one person, on average. They did not give me a specific number. However, they did tell me that **one in five interviewees (20%) who make it to the loop interview usually get an offer.**

From my experience, this holds true. If I had a handful of four to five people interviewing for one job, then the hiring managers would have a good enough sample size to compare different interviewees and make a decision.

Now, take note that this does **not** factor in the number of people who apply or the number of people who go from screening interview to the loop interview.

I would say a similar number of people got rejected at the application screening stage, but slightly less after the first interview. Usually, if you get to the first interview, you are meeting the hiring manager. They have the biggest incentive to hire and tend to push people through the process.

With that said the probabilities of getting hired looks something like this:

- one in five chance to get an interview from the resume screening stage
- one in two chance to go from the first interview to loop (generous hiring managers)
- one in five chance to go from loop to offer

So, ten people apply for the job, two people get an interview, one of those go to loop and 20% of them are likely to get the job. As you can see, this has to happen a few times. Of course, there were exceptions to this, and for one executive-level hire I worked on, the position remained open for two years - more than 12 people went to the loop interview with no hire.

There are also exceptions that go the other way. Usually, the more junior the position is, the easier it is to fill. So things can go a lot faster in some cases, like five loop interviews and two hires that come out of that (in which case there might be only two to three people in the loop interview).

Do not get too discouraged by these numbers. They are averages, and I am certain that a majority of people that have interviewed have not taken a significant amount of time to prepare well for the interviews. This already gives you a big advantage and opportunity to be one of the lucky 20% who receives an offer.

However, Amazon is not an easy company to impress. You should remain humble and if things do not work out the first time, realize that you can apply for other positions in the future. Amazon keeps the door open to people who want to re-apply in the future.

CHAPTER 12:

COMPENSATION AND SALARY NEGOTIATION

Amazon's salary structure is fairly straightforward and has remained pretty consistent over the years. Amazon uses a mix of guaranteed cash and stock to incentivize employees. There are three components.

1. Base Salary
2. Guaranteed Bonus
3. Restricted Stock Units ("RSUs" that vest over a four year period)[1]

Let's break down a hypothetical offer Amazon would give:

Base Pay Offered: $120,000
Sign-on Payment Year 1: $40,000
Sign-on Payment Year 2: $40,000
Shares of RSUs offered: 100

This means you will receive a guaranteed compensation of $160,000 the first two years (bonuses paid over a period of 12 months + base pay).

---

[1] A restricted stock unit is compensation offered by an employer to an employee in the form of company stock. The employee does not receive the stock immediately, but instead receives it according to a vesting plan and distribution schedule after achieving required performance milestones or upon remaining with the employer for a particular length of time.

From the third year of employment your "guaranteed bonus" drops. Instead, you will be rewarded with shares of the company.

The RSUs vest over four years and you receive 100% of these by the end of year four. Here is the vesting period:

- first year: 5% of RSUs
- second year 15% of RSUs
- third year: 40% of RSUs
- fourth year: the remaining 40% of RSUs

Here is an *estimate* what you would make the first four years (with Amazon stock price at $1,000/share, 100 RSUs being equal to $100,000 over four years):

Year 1: $120k base + $40k Sign on Bonus + 5% RSUs (5K) = $165k

Year 2: $120k base + $40k Sign on Bonus + 15% RSUs (15K) = $175k

Year 3: $120k base + 40% RSUs (40K) = $160K

Year 4: $120k base + 40% RSUs (40K) = $160K

As you will notice, your compensation comprised of your base and bonus might go down after the third year which can seem surprising. However, do not be alarmed, as historically wages don't go down. Why? Because Amazon's stock has done phenomenally well. Just a couple of years ago it was at $300 and has more than tripled since to $1,000 per share. The assumption is that the stock price will go up, and your hard work and dedication is contributing to that.

The above structure also does not take into consideration potential pay raise you can get or the fluctuation in stock price (up or down). Most people get a raise in salary or more stock after year one or two, so this can easily go up.

Salary Negotiation

You should first determine what parts of the salary are important for you. Amazon naturally prefers to award more Restricted Stock Units because it shows your longer-term commitment to the company. However, if your preference is to get a higher base or sign-on bonus, you should be very clear about this going into the interview process. Keep in mind that Amazon tends to have pretty set budgets for their positions, so there is only so far that you can stretch the base.

The biggest faux-pas is requesting only to have a base and bonus salary. This simply isn't possible, and Amazon always gives a mix of the three pieces as mentioned above. Furthermore, if you de-emphasize the RSU component, it will make the negative impression that you're just there for the short term, which can create issues. Amazon does not frequently rescind their offers, but I have seen it happen.

Amazon HR is not likely to talk about your salary in the early stages of the interview. If they *do* start talking about your salary range early on in the process, it may mean that you received really good feedback (and they want to make sure they keep you interested). Or they think you might be overqualified, based on your current compensation, so they are double checking before conducting all of the interviews. Typically salary conversations are saved until after the loop interview.

There are a couple of ways to approach the negotiation process. You can either take a more passive approach or a more active approach. Which one you choose will depend on your *current* salary.

Passive Approach. You should use this approach if you think that you are being underpaid in your current job. For example, let's say that you are currently making $40,000 per year in your job. You have received an offer for an L5 position at Amazon, which according to the rough ranges which I explained above, would pay somewhere between $60,000-$100,000 at the very top end.

No matter what salary Amazon decides to give you, it's almost certain that it is going to be a big step up for you. You don't need to tell Amazon your current salary. In this situation, you also don't likely need to "fight" for a good salary. In fact, you don't really need to do much except wait for the offer. Indeed, whatever salary they give you is a step up. However, you can still tell Amazon HR your preferences for the split, i.e., whether you would prefer more base, sign-on bonuses, or RSU's.

Active Approach. You should use this approach if you are unsure if you can get a competitive salary from Amazon. For example, if you are currently making $90,000 and get an offer for a L5 position, then it's unclear whether or not you are going to be able to get a raise. This means that you need to be on the offensive and proactively disclose to your Amazon recruiter your current compensation and your desired compensation. When moving companies a good increase in salary is a 10-20% gain. Anything higher than this is considered quite a big jump.

You should be very clear what the minimum salary is that you'd like to have per year. Remember, the sign on bonus is split over a 12 month period and is guaranteed. The RSUs kick in from the second year. Whenever you give them your proposal for *expected salary,* naturally you should start high.

It's very possible that your base salary actually goes down when joining Amazon because of the way they structure their compensation. You should go in expecting this. This often shocks people because they simply don't understand the compensation structure. Keep in mind that *everyone at Amazon is paid under the same structure* so they are not going to make an exception for you. Fortunately, you won't be surprised by this, because you know what to expect. Remember that the RSUs have historically done very well and salaries at Amazon take an upward trajectory, as long as you stay there.

I'd like to express one word of caution about tying your perceived value in the market to your salary. This effect has been tested in psychology quite extensively, that is, people experience far more mental anguish and pain when they perceive a loss of something they already have, compared to a much lesser pain from a gain that they never receive. For example, if you don't get that promotion and 10% salary increase you were expecting, it won't be fun. But it's going to be *far more* painful if you get a 10% *decrease* from your current salary.

While it's hard to break free from our psychological tendencies, we should recognize that compensation is only one piece of the puzzle. If you are excited about the job, believe that you can contribute to the company, and gain valuable experience in the meantime, then salary should not be your top priority. I understand that people have mortgages and bills to pay -- naturally, they should factor in all of their expenses. However, I have seen many people reject offers because they didn't get that small bump in salary that they wanted, most of which would be eaten by taxes anyways. In sum, take a moment to consider your true reasons for wanting to leave your job and make sure you are clear on your priorities.

Lastly, if you are relocating cross-country or internationally, Amazon uses third party vendors that will handle your entire move from you. This includes visa support. Typically the relocation allowance is equivalent to one or two months of your base salary. If your base is $80,000, then you'd get a package between $6,000 and $12,000 to relocate depending on how many family members you have.

CHAPTER 13:

PERSPECTIVES FROM AMAZON HIRING MANAGERS

Product Management

"When hiring product managers, I generally look for people with proven track record of delivering customer value. Has this person identified a customer problem, and a solution, built it, and launched it? I find that the most successful product managers at Amazon show relentless focus on customer metrics to inform data-based prioritization, and a bias for action to deliver features. Lastly, I am looking for leaders. Does this person have the ability to inspire a vision for their team? Can this person be trusted by their team? Will this person do everything, not just tasks in their job description, for their team to be successful?"

-Abhay Saxena, Principal of Alexa's Voice Shopping platform

Program Management

"In 2012, I was asked to manage a technology project for Zappos, an Amazon subsidiary with its own <u>unique culture and core values that govern it</u>, a culture that is polar opposite from that of Amazon. I took on this role with the assumption that I would learn more about technology and how to manage engineers. However, during the next two years what I experienced was a living case study on human psychology and organizational culture. I became a bridge between the left brain of Amazon and the right brain of Zappos, observing pros and cons of each organization's philosophy on how to work. I was able to learn the languages of both, and my ability to translate Amazon speak into Zappos speak, and vice versa, was critical to removing roadblocks and making progress. I learned that every collaborative effort - regardless of the subject matter - boils down to people and what motivates them.

Taking this learning further, I started to wonder: Could a company merge the principles and values from Amazon and Zappos to create a culture that is both data-driven and empathetic in parallel? Could an organization with this hypothetical culture also enable each person to contribute to a company's success while achieving a sense of personal fulfillment and happiness? What happens when you give the tin man a heart?

I truly believe a culture such as this - a culture that embraces the head and the heart, values data as much as empathy, marrying technology and humanity - is feasible. More so, I believe it is the sustainable framework in which an organization can operate to achieve both short *and* long-term success, for customers, shareholders, *and* employees."

-*Dina Vaccari, Program Manager Retail Integration*

Engineering

"When I interviewed at Amazon, I heard all the horror stories from the past. They're actually pretty well known in Seattle. I was told they were true, that the company continues to take steps to make things better, and that work-life balance was taken seriously. I wasn't convinced, but I took a bet because I wanted to work on Computational Theory problems and Distributed Systems at scale that can only be found at Amazon. Here's my experience:

During my 18 months at Amazon, I've never worked a single weekend when I didn't want to. No one tells me to work nights. No one makes me answer emails at night. No one texts me to ask me why emails aren't answered. I don't have these expectations of the managers that work for me, and if they were to do this to their Engineers, I would rectify that myself, immediately. And if these expectations were in place, and enforced upon me, I would leave."

-Nick Ciubotariu, Sr. Software Developer Amazon

Recruitment

When asked, "Can you give me an example of a time when ..." think back on the stories you have told about your work experiences. And for each, think about the beginning, the middle and the end. What was the situation you encountered? Paint the picture for me, was it a business challenge that was unexpected? How did you navigate it, what did you learn and how did you help champion others in that process? Give me important details – but not unnecessary verbosity – so I understand how many layers you peeled to figure out the root cause of the problem. Tell me how you persevered. Show me your character, your grit, your moxie! Then, tell me how the story ends. People who are artful behavioral based interviewers often bring the story full circle by saying, "and then this is the impact it had on the business ...". Be a storyteller.

-Jeanne Skinner, Sr. Leadership Recruitment

Innovation

Invention requires a long-term willingness to be misunderstood. You do something that you genuinely believe in, that you have conviction about, but for a long period of time, well- meaning people may criticize that effort. When you receive criticism from well-meaning people, it pays to ask, 'Are they right?' And if they are, you need to adapt what they're doing. If they're not right, if you really have conviction that they're not right, you need to have that long-term willingness to be misunderstood. It's a key part of invention.

- Jeff Bezos

Fulfillment Centers

Yes, there are days where I hate my job. I wonder at the intelligence of some of my co- workers, I'm amazed at the laziness of others, I go home exhausted from a 10-hour shift, and I sometimes feel like some members of the leadership team don't recognize my contributions. *But* this has been one of the best warehouse jobs I've had. I have done some of the same things here (making and filling boxes) for $4.50/hr less (minimum wage) at other places. I have been allowed to really showcase my extra skills and knowledge in my work here. The work can really be as diverse as you want it to be. We have a lot of different jobs that can be done within my department (over 100 individual processes) related to testing the functionality and grading standards for each device and associates can be rotated through all of these (with training obviously).

Amazon is the only place I've heard of that's willing to take someone off the street (given they can pass a drug test) and believe they can learn anything. Our department is very heavily computer-based. We have people that came in here knowing very little to nothing about computers and because they were given a chance and a little training, they are excelling.

-Jennifer Schnoor, Warehouse Associate

Internships

I was an SDE intern in Amazon Seattle during the summer of 2016, and I'm currently a return intern for this term. I had an amazing time during my last internship, and I'm looking forward to the experience for the winter.

You can likely expect to get a challenging, self-contained project to work on for your months there. My project was well scoped, and I got to spend some thinking about (and improving) my design. My teammates were also really helpful with reviewing both my documents and code - which helped me learn a ton. You'll get assigned a mentor that you can talk to daily who's familiar with your project space, and have weekly 1-on-1s with your manager. During the summer, there's a lot of intern events (and a lot of interns), so it's likely that you'll find some fun things to do.

I thought that a huge plus side of internships at Amazon is the amount of ownership you get over your project. If you don't want to be the one driving your project, then that aspect may be a con for you.

-Abrar Hussain, Software Development intern

Data

'In God we trust. The rest please bring data.' This is a profile signature of an Amazon employee. I think it summarizes Amazon's obsession with analytics quite well.

I left Amazon a few years ago, after working there as a product manager for 2.5 years. Based on my observation, the job was quite analytical, dealing with Excel all the time and SQL occasionally. In fact, I always recommend people interested in working at Amazon to familiarize themselves with SQL and Excel. If you are good at both of them, you will be more likely to get hired, but more importantly, your life will be less miserable after you join. Once one of my coworkers was overwhelmed by the demanding data analysis tasks and suggested we hire a data analyst to help. The answer he got was: "We already have several data analysts on the team. It's just that they are called product managers here at Amazon."

I've been with companies where data is hard to come by and many decisions become "boss- centered", i.e., whatever the manager likes is the right way to go. At Amazon, it is quite different. After the financial crisis broke out in 2008, the retail outlook became worse. Being more careful with marketing spending, Amazon decided to cut their budget in search advertising, very significantly, across all categories. With data, I was able to convince the company to revisit the decision. We eventually raised the spending target back for three categories.

-Boris Shen, Product Manager

Don't automatically assume that everybody at Amazon is good at numbers though. There are always exceptions. A colleague of mine had told me a horror story. He once presented his Excel spreadsheet, filled with rigorous logic, to his manager. During the one-hour discussion, the feedback he got was all like this: "I think you should increase the font size to 12. " or "I think the line in that graph will look better in red."

The First 90 Days on the Job

"Here are some tips reflecting my personal experience:

- **Leverage your onboarding period.** This is the only period, where you can be "non-productive" and ask many questions to your on-boarding buddy. Take advantage of it and learn as much as possible. Later on, when you will have more work than free time (this is common in Amazon), you will thank yourself that you are up to speed with all the tools and processes and you can spend your time on actual work.
- **Earn trust.** Yes, I know this might sound a bit "cult", since this is one of the LPs of Amazon. However, it's extremely important. In order to have impact, you need people to trust you with important projects, etc. To achieve that, try to complete any task assigned to you with the best possible result, attend meetings having already read relevant material, so that you can participate and contribute.
- **Be open to criticism.** You will receive criticism for your work frequently. People try to deliver the best result; they don't have anything personal with you. So, try to learn as much as possible from this and improve yourself.
- **Use data.** For every decision you have to make, explore all alternatives, their pros and cons and then make your suggestion based on data. People will try to challenge your choice, so be prepared to explain why it's the best.
- **Embrace chaos.** Amazon is a fast-moving company. As a result, there might be big reorganizations and team changes; people might leave your team, etc. This might seem chaotic at first, but it's a great opportunity. Think positively. Leverage team changes to educate yourself

about new business domains and network with new people. Leverage people leaving the team with fewer resources, by owning systems and tasks left "orphaned."

- **Chill out.** There are many fun events organizes across Amazon, such as parties, sports teams, communities, etc. Take your time off, stop thinking about work and try to have fun with some co-workers.

My experience comes mainly from Software Engineering at Amazon. However, I tried to be as generic as possible, so that the tips can be helpful to any role."

Cheers and have a great start!"

-Dimos Raptis, Software Engineer

Customer Obsession

"Jeff Bezos, founder of *Amazon.com*, while learning about *'Books' Business'* wanted to learn *'How to Sell Books.'* So he attended an introductory four day lecture in Portland by *American Bookseller Association*. During that he met one of the instructors named Richard Howorth. Richard told him the story of how far you've to go for customer service.

One day, while Richard was in his office of the bookstore, the manager came to him and told that one lady was ridiculously argumentative about something.

'You gotta come and deal with her, Richard!' he told him.

So Richard went downstairs and asked, 'How may I help you?'

'Well, my car was parked outside *your* store, when the guy in the balcony of the flat threw mud on my car from upstairs. My husband cleaned up my car just this morning. Who's gonna clean it now?' asked the lady.

'Can I wash your car?' asked Richard, to which she said: "Yes, please." And both of them drove to a nearby car-cleaning service, which unfortunately was closed that day. Richard then said, 'Let's go to my home.' and they drove to his home.

Richard Howorth, a senior instructor at ABA, who was the owner of one of the largest Bookstore in the county, and owner of *Square Book* in Mississippi right now, took a bucket of water and a rag from his garage and cleaned her car.

Jeff Bezos, founder of Amazon.com, said "That day I realized how far you have to go to please a customer. And then I decided to make sure Amazon was customer-centric."

-Nikhil Patel, Software Developer

Amazon vs. Google

"Search Advertising

Google clearly dominates the web search market, and Amazon is not a direct competitor in the general domain. However, when people search for a new razor or lawn mower or shampoo or whatnot, they could search on Google – or they could search directly on Amazon.

In either case, brands and manufacturers would love to have their product show up high, and that happens organically (because the search engine believes your page is one of the most relevant ones). Or because you agreed to pay for clicks and have your ad shown, marked as an ad (and again depending on the decision of the engine, this time the ad one).

Amazon is certainly behind AdWords in terms of sophistication and flexibility, but they have one very nice advantage: an ad click may lead to a page and then directly to a sale, on Amazon, which Amazon can record and attribute to the ad. Google has to work much harder to get information about what happened after the click and is often unable to do so at all.

Many brands, including some very large ones, are increasingly using Amazon search marketing, and some of those marketing dollars may come at the expense of more traditional search engine marketing.

Smart Homes

Amazon Echo and Google Home are directly competing for the privilege of responding to your vocal utterances in your own home. This is a fairly new market, but both companies are taking it very seriously. Some 60 million people in the US are expected to use such a device at least once a month this year.

Shopping and Delivery

Amazon's focus on shopping and home delivery needs no introduction. In some areas of the US, Google Express offers to do your Costco, Target or Walmart shopping for you and deliver the goods to your home. My impression is that this isn't a viable long-term business for Google, but I may be wrong about that. At any rate, it's competition.

Subscription Video-on-Demand

In 2016 YouTube, which has been free for over a decade, moved into paid, ad-free, original- content land with YouTube Red. For $12.99 a month you get free music, offline videos and original productions from YouTube.

As a free product supporting ad revenue, YouTube has been very successful. The Red version is more nascent, and revenue is still very small compared with ad revenue from standard YouTube, and time will tell if and how fast it grows. The competition on Amazon's side is Amazon Prime Video, which piggybacks on the popular Amazon Prime subscription. Both companies are obviously in direct competition with Netflix and Hulu, two companies for which this is the main business. TechCrunch reported some data on market share earlier this year: Netflix was leading, followed by YouTube and then Amazon.

Finally, I'm reminded of something I read in 2004 or thereabouts. It was an interview with Bill Gates, then still the head of the world's leading hi-tech company, Microsoft. He was asked about Google as a competitor.

Instead of dismissing them off-hand as a lesser leader would do, Gates responded that Google is a clear and direct competitor, or even a threat – not because they do Search, but because they are a software company. Gates identified Google's prominence among software engineers and correctly recognized them as a threat to his own company which led the software world for decades. He was right to be worried.

Companies compete on more than specific products. They compete on overall leadership, prominence, brand value, and hiring. On all of these fronts, Amazon and Google (as well as Facebook and Apple) are currently in direct competition."

-Along Amit, Product Manager

CHAPTER 14:

ROCK N' ROLL!

You can use this checklist to prepare for your meeting with Amazon.

1. The Amazon "Flywheel" business model is key to understanding how they operate. Always keep in mind the different levers when answering interview questions.
2. Amazon looks for certain keywords in resumes. Make sure you include these in your resume and furthermore understand the job level you are applying for.
3. The 14 leadership principles are at the core of Amazon's culture. Interviewers will test every single one. Make sure to prepare four to five detailed examples based on these principles.
4. Use the STAR Method to structure and answer questions in a logical way.
5. Avoid common pitfalls. Always answer the question, know your examples in detail, and don't be afraid to share your failure stories.
6. Understand the salary levels and be ready to actively negotiate if necessary.
7. Use the tools in front of you! This information gives you a huge advantage. Now all you need to do is to prepare.

CONCLUSION

Interviews are not easy and Amazon is notoriously difficult to get into. Difficult, but not impossible. I've found that job seekers who spent the most time preparing did the best, regardless of their background. Like a standardized test, interviewing is a learned skill. This may seem simplistic, but with other priorities and our lives to live, it can be surprisingly hard to do. While interviews may only take up 4-5 hours of time the preparation and research you will do, it will take much longer.

With that said, I hope this book has given you a good starting point for your preparation, application and interviews with Amazon. If you found it useful, I would greatly appreciate you taking 1 minute to leave a review on Amazon.

You can check out my blog at www.mishayurchenko.me for more interview tips and tools. Also, feel free to reach out to me anytime with more specific questions or comments.

Until next time and good luck!

USEFUL LINKS

Finally, I would like to share some useful books, videos, and links related to Amazon that I recommend.

The Everything Store: Jeff Bezos and the Age of Amazon by Brad Stone

Amazon Leadership Principles: https://www.amazon.jobs/principles

The Amazon Way: 14 Leadership Principles Behind the World's Most Disruptive Company by John Rossman

STAR Interview Method: https://starinterviewmethod.com/

Extreme Ownership by Jocko Willink

Breakdown by David Anderson URL: https://www.linkedin.com/pulse/how-interview-amazon-leadership-david-anderson/

Amazonian HR Blog: http://www.amazonianblog.com/

Videos:

https://www.youtube.com/watch?v=pEZqCuEEMdU
http://www.youtube.com/watch?v=kTM4pDdvqrU
http://www.youtube.com/watch?v=_KEKkVrzeU8
http://www.youtube.com/watch?v=zgdeeple--o
Jeff Bezos Interview Videos: URL https://bit.ly/2pL8Y7G

One-on-one career consulting

If you'd like to get feedback on your resume or have questions about interviewing at Amazon, I provide a 1-1 consulting service. We can discuss the following:

- Your plan for applying to certain recruitment companies and whether it's the right move.
- Honest feedback on your resume with specific tips to improve.
- Interview tips, feedback, and objective advice on any pending offers you have.

And whatever other questions you have related to your job search

You can schedule a time to speak with me via this link: https://bit.ly/2A1vz5M

Contact:

You can reach out to me via my blog and follow me for updates at www.mishayurchenko.me

29972184R00057

Printed in Great
Britain
by Amazon